MW01247773

Let's Speak Spanish
second edition A

Conrad J. Schmitt

Webster Division, McGraw-Hill Book Company

New York • St. Louis • San Francisco • Auckland • Bogotá • Düsseldorf
Johannesburg • London • Madrid • Mexico • Montreal • New Delhi • Panama
Paris • São Paulo • Singapore • Sydney • Tokyo • Toronto

Editor: Teresa Chimienti
Editing Supervisor: Alice Jaggard
Design: Lisa Delgado Pagani
Production Supervisor: Salvador Gonzales

Illustrations: Tony Rao

Library of Congress Cataloging in Publication Data

Schmitt, Conrad J
  Let's speak Spanish, A.

  Part of an audio-lingual-visual program which consists
of a teacher's manual, a pupil's edition, cue cards, and
cassettes.
  Includes index.
  SUMMARY: This first book in a four-volume series for
learning Spanish in the elementary school consists of
drawings and places the emphasis on listening and speaking.
  1. Spanish language—Grammar—1950– —Juvenile
literature. [1. Spanish language—Grammar] I. Title.
PC4112.S356 1978   372.6'5'61   77-8914
ISBN 0-07-055481-1

Copyright ©1978, 1964 by McGraw-Hill, Inc. All Rights Reserved. Printed in
the United States of America. No part of this publication may be reproduced,
stored in a retrieval system, or transmitted, in any form or by any
means, electronic, mechanical, photocopying, recording, or otherwise,
without the prior written permission of the publisher.

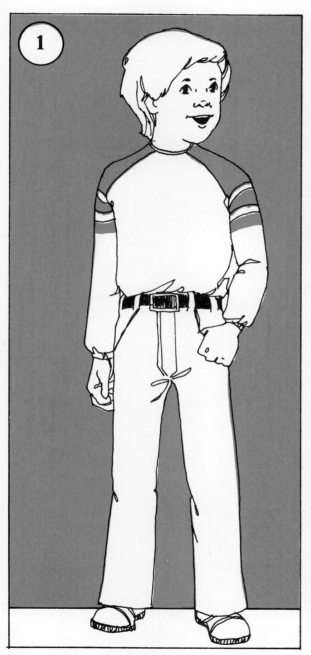

LESSON 2

2

5

6

6

LESSON 3

LESSON 4

LESSON 5

28

30

1

2

36

37

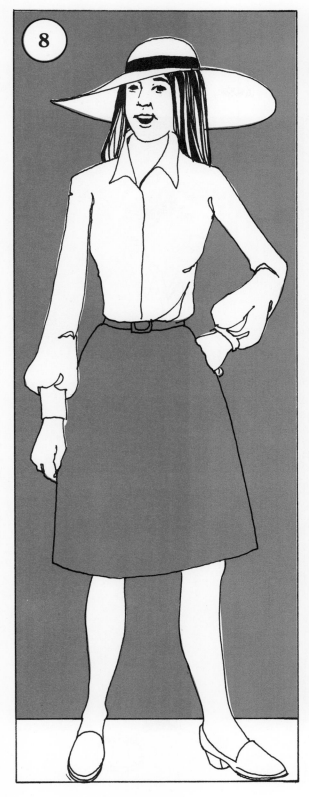

LESSON 8

43

46

LESSON 9

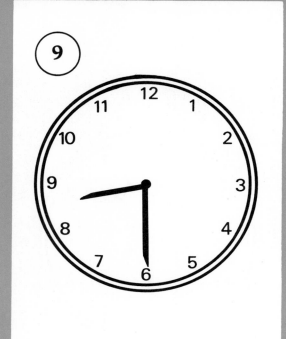

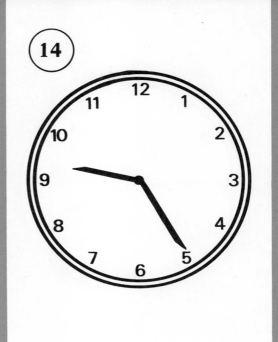

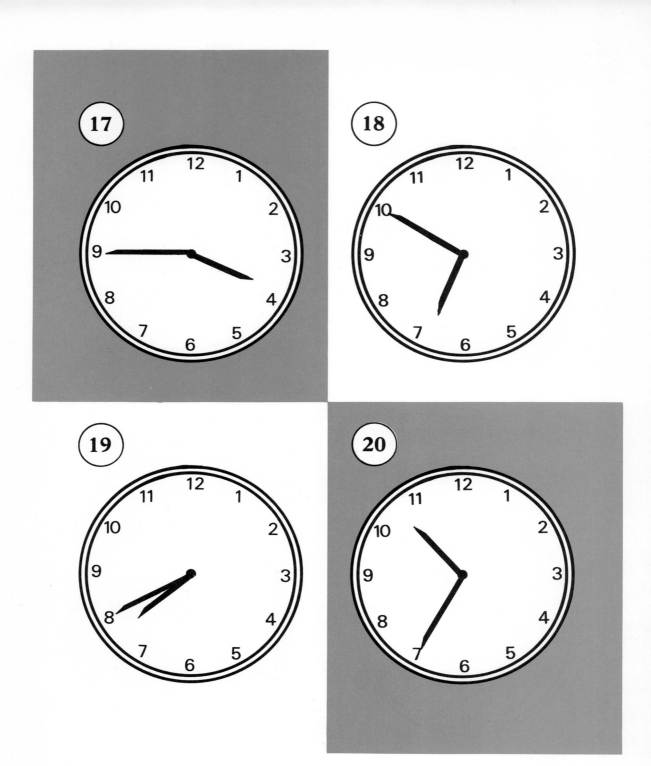

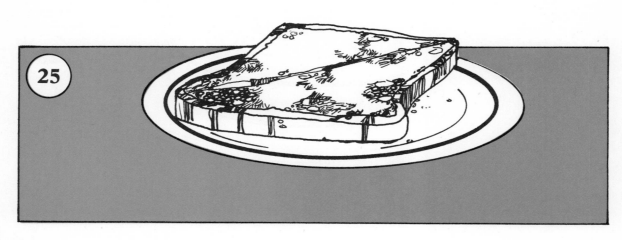

56

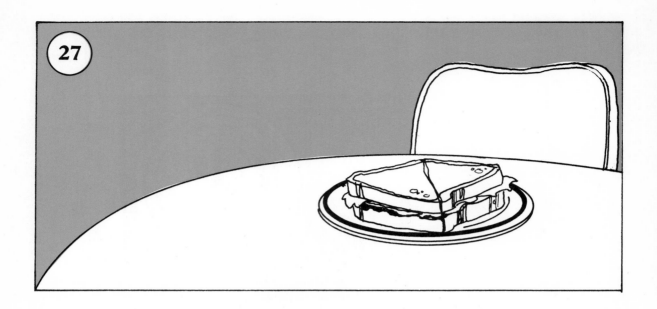

58

35

63

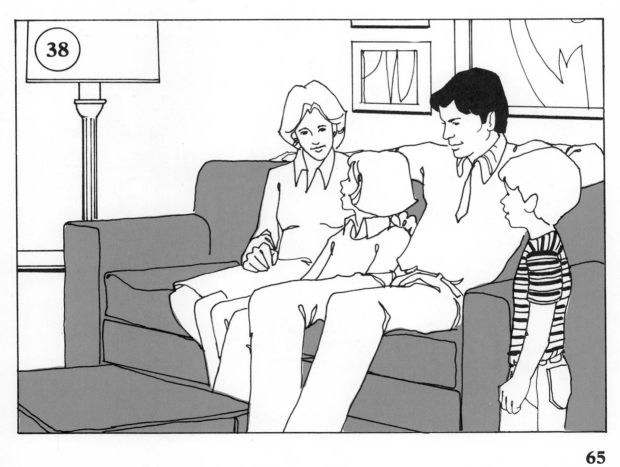

65

LESSON 10

67

75